GW01338937

Christopher Rawlins CE Primary School
Aynho Road, Adderbury OX17 3NH

WILL YOU BE MY FRIEND, PEACOCK?

A story of true friendship

Written by
Rohini Krishnapura

Illustrated by
Csongor Veres

Copyright © 2021. Boxinthemiddle LLC

All rights reserved. No part of this publication may be reproduced, distributed, or transmitted in any form or by any means, including photocopying, recording, or other electronic or mechanical methods, without the prior written permission of the publisher, except in the case of brief quotations embodied in critical reviews and certain other noncommercial uses permitted by copyright law.

ISBN: 978-1-7364736-0-3

Published by Boxinthemiddle LLC
www.boxinthemiddle.com

This is for:

Sanica,, the reason this story was created, 9 years ago.

Sunchit, my little boy, for always believing in Mom.

Kumar, for staying at my side through all my transformations.

Once upon a time, in a garden far away, there lived a beautiful peacock. This peacock had beautiful feathers and he knew it! Everyday, the peacock would spread his feathers to dance and show his colorful plumage. People travelled from far places to see this beautiful peacock dance and they marvelled at his feathers.

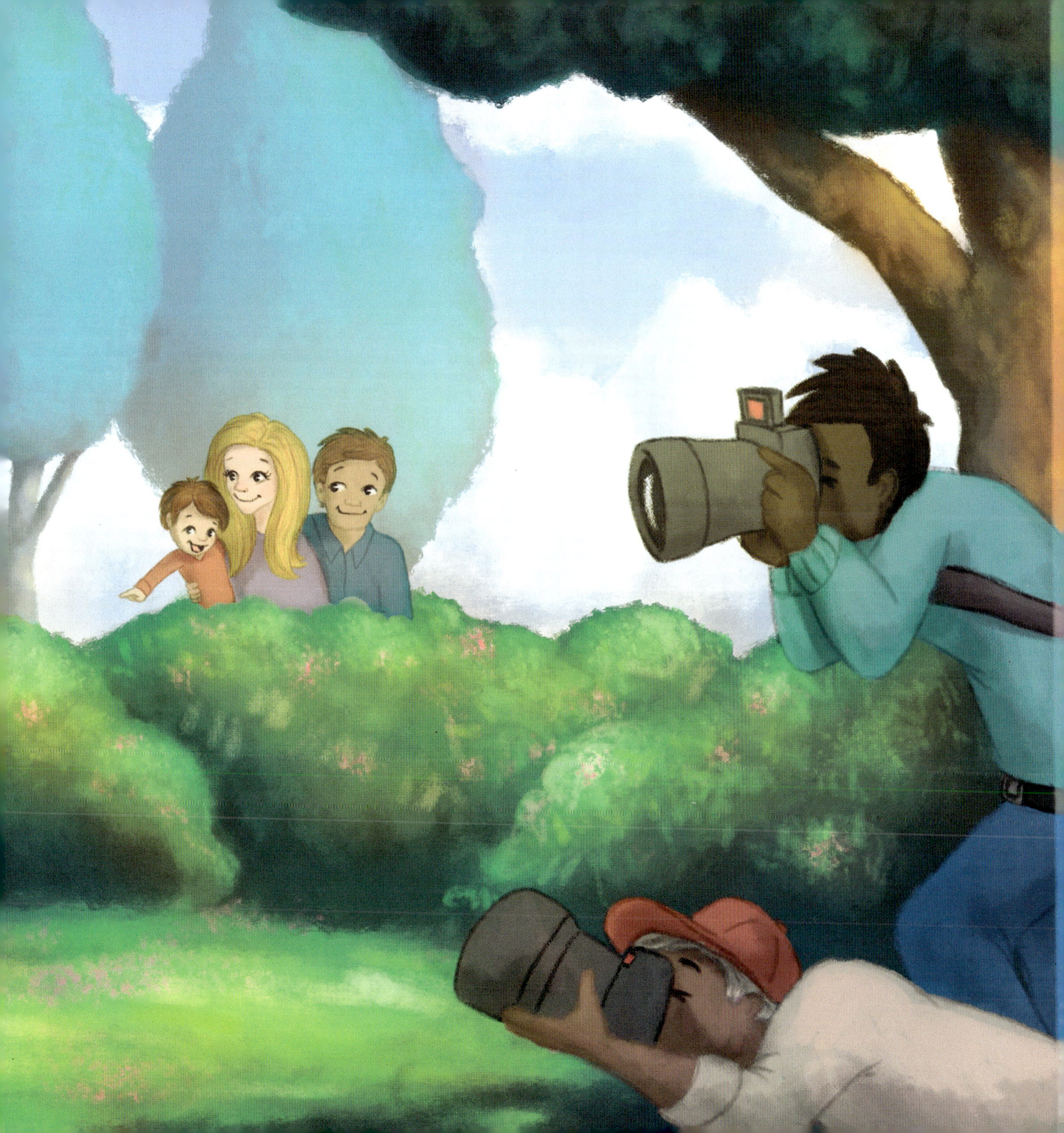

In the same garden, lived another, younger peacock whose feathers weren't fully developed yet. The younger peacock ever so wanted to be friends with the older peacock.

One day, the younger peacock saw the older peacock sitting on a stump, basking in the sun and pruning his beautiful feathers. As the sun rays bounced off the striking colors of his feathers, he looked quite majestic.

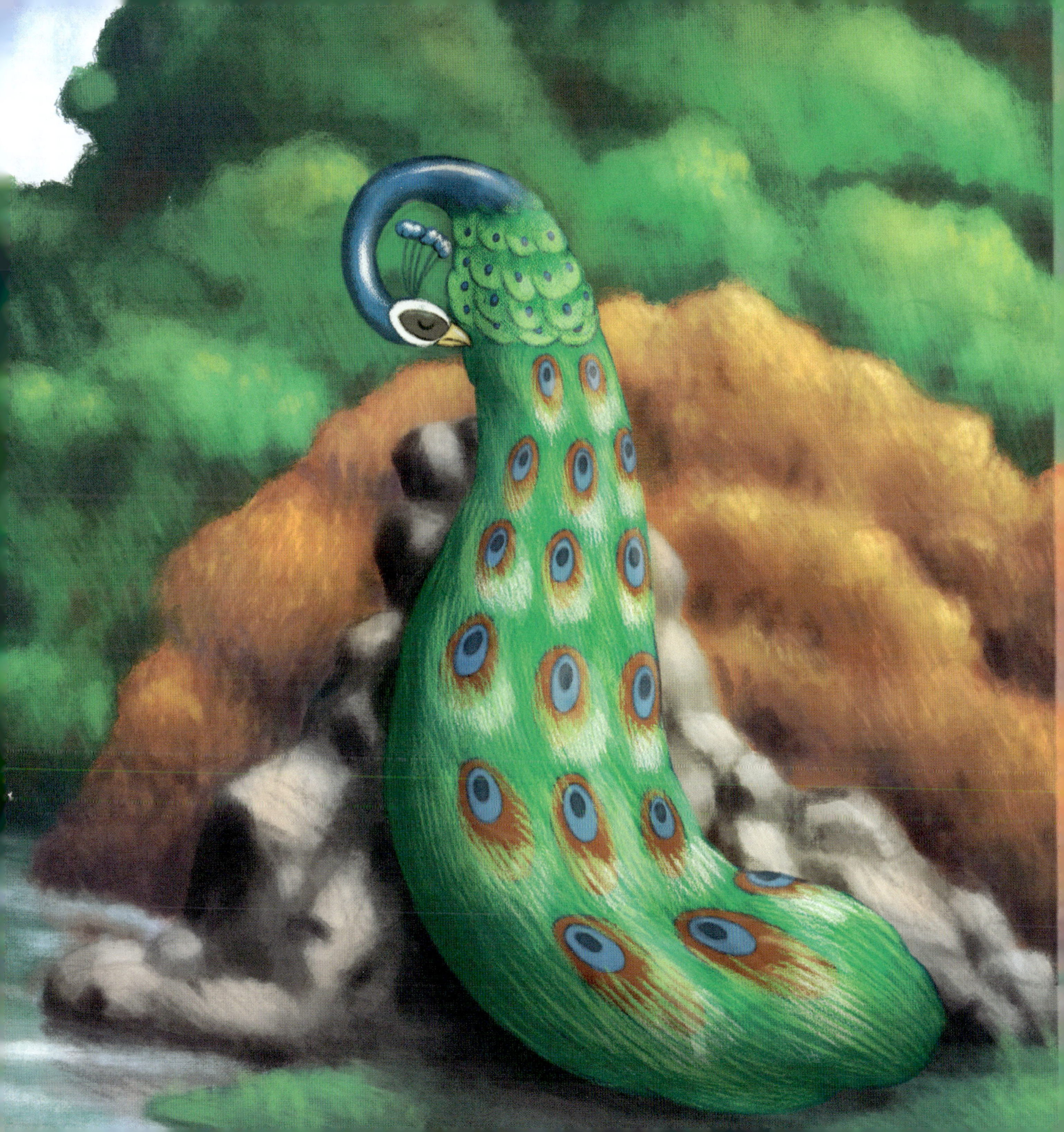

So, the younger peacock walked up to him, mustered up a lot of courage and said, "Hi......mmm..., can we be friends?" At first, the older peacock didn't even hear him and so he had to repeat himself. "Hello? Will you be my friend?"

Finally, the older peacock looked up lazily and said,

"I don't have time to be friends with you. Do you know who I am? *Everyone* comes to see my beautiful dance. I have to keep my feathers clean and I have to practice. Don't bother me now….shoo".

The younger peacock was hurt. But, he didn't give up. Everyday, he would ask to be friends and everyday the older peacock shooed him away.

Mon 🕛

"Good morning sleepyhead! You know what they say about the early bird catching the worm? Here you go. Now, will you be my friend?"

Tue 🕐

"Oooh....darlin'.....I love your feathers today!. What did you do? You must tell me... you absolutely must!"

"Oh really? I did start brushing differently...didn't think anyone would notice...the trick is to..."

"So, will you be my friend?"

Wed

"*Boo!!*
Will you be my friend?"

Thu

"Isn't it such a beautiful day today? Y'know what'd make it better? You and me...pals....eh?"

Fri 🕛 "TGIF right? Phew! Brutal week….I'm telling ya"
"We should catch up over the weekend. What do you think, mate?"

Sat 🕝 "Hey bro! Catching some rad waves, man! You in?"

"Hi buddy! How about a sleepover?"

Sun

One day, a hungry fox wandered into the garden. He hadn't eaten for days! He hid in the bushes and spotted the two peacocks. "Mmmm, yummy. he mumbled as his tummy rumbled."

He inched closer to the peacocks and saw that the older peacock was too busy to notice. But, the younger peacock felt that something was wrong and saw the fox. He rushed over to the other peacock and said, "I have to tell you something. I have to tell you something now! It's really urgent".

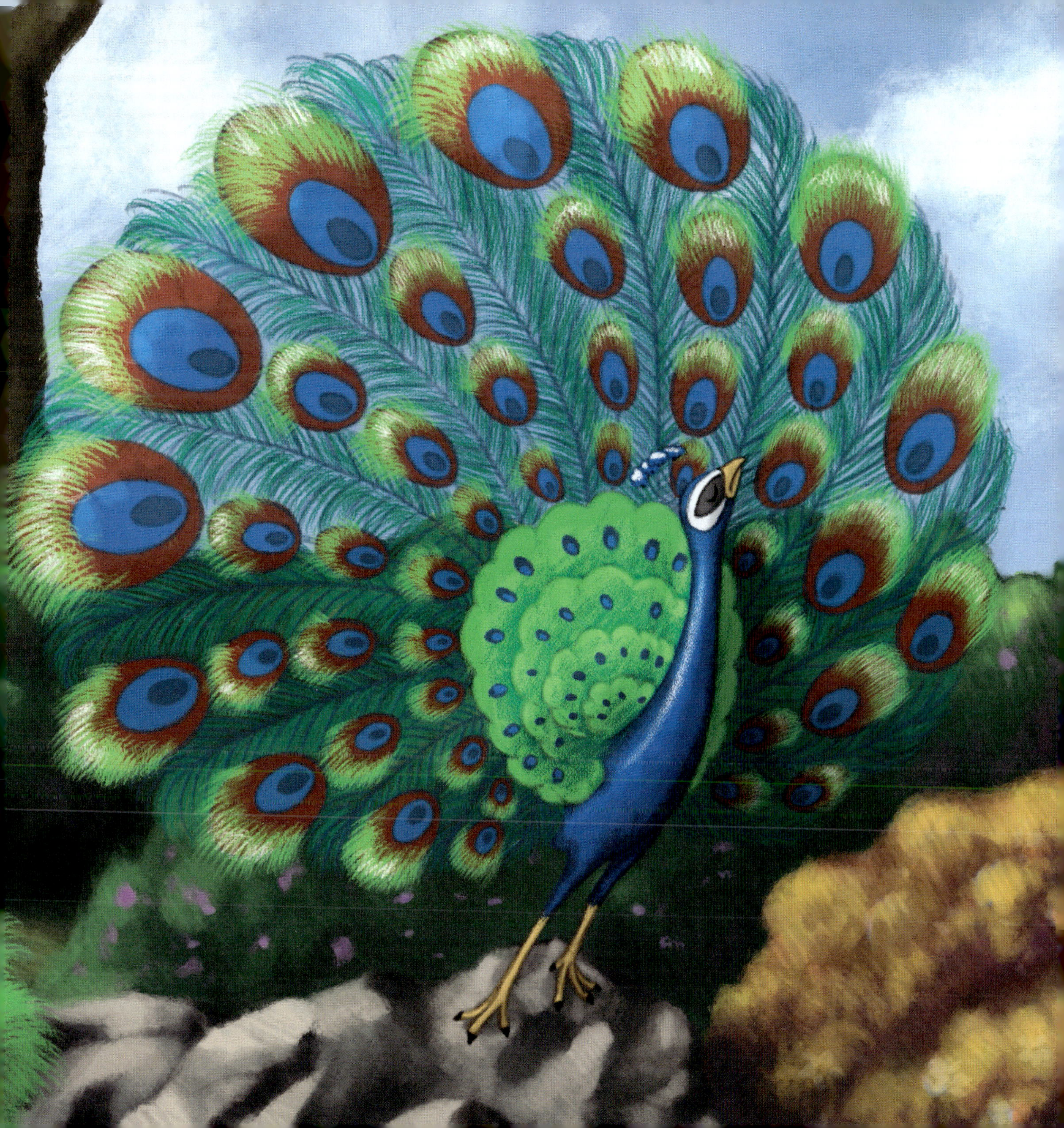

But, the older peacock turned his back to him and shooed him away. Meanwhile, the fox had moved closer. The younger peacock tried again to warn the older peacock,

"You have to listen to me! There's something in the bushes!."

"Stop bothering me everyday. Of course, there's something in the bushes. This is a garden. It's probably some squirrels or birds playing in the bushes. Leave me alone.", frowned the older peacock.

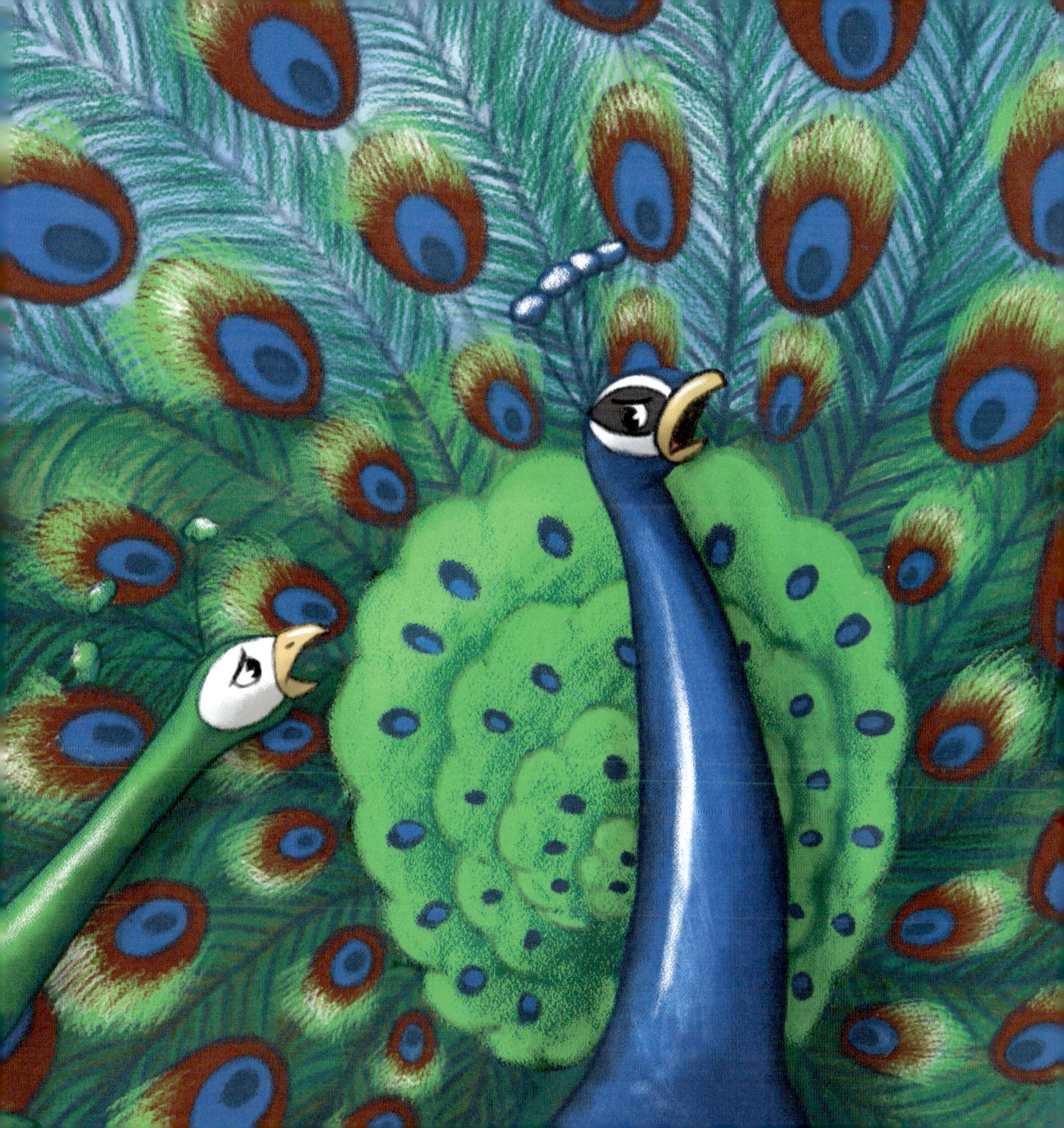

Now, the fox was ever so close. As the younger peacock tried again, it was too late. The fox leapt out of the bushes and attacked the older peacock. The older peacock fought well but the fox was strong and had taken him by surprise. The younger peacock was scared. But, as he saw the older peacock getting hurt, he jumped in to help in spite of his fear.

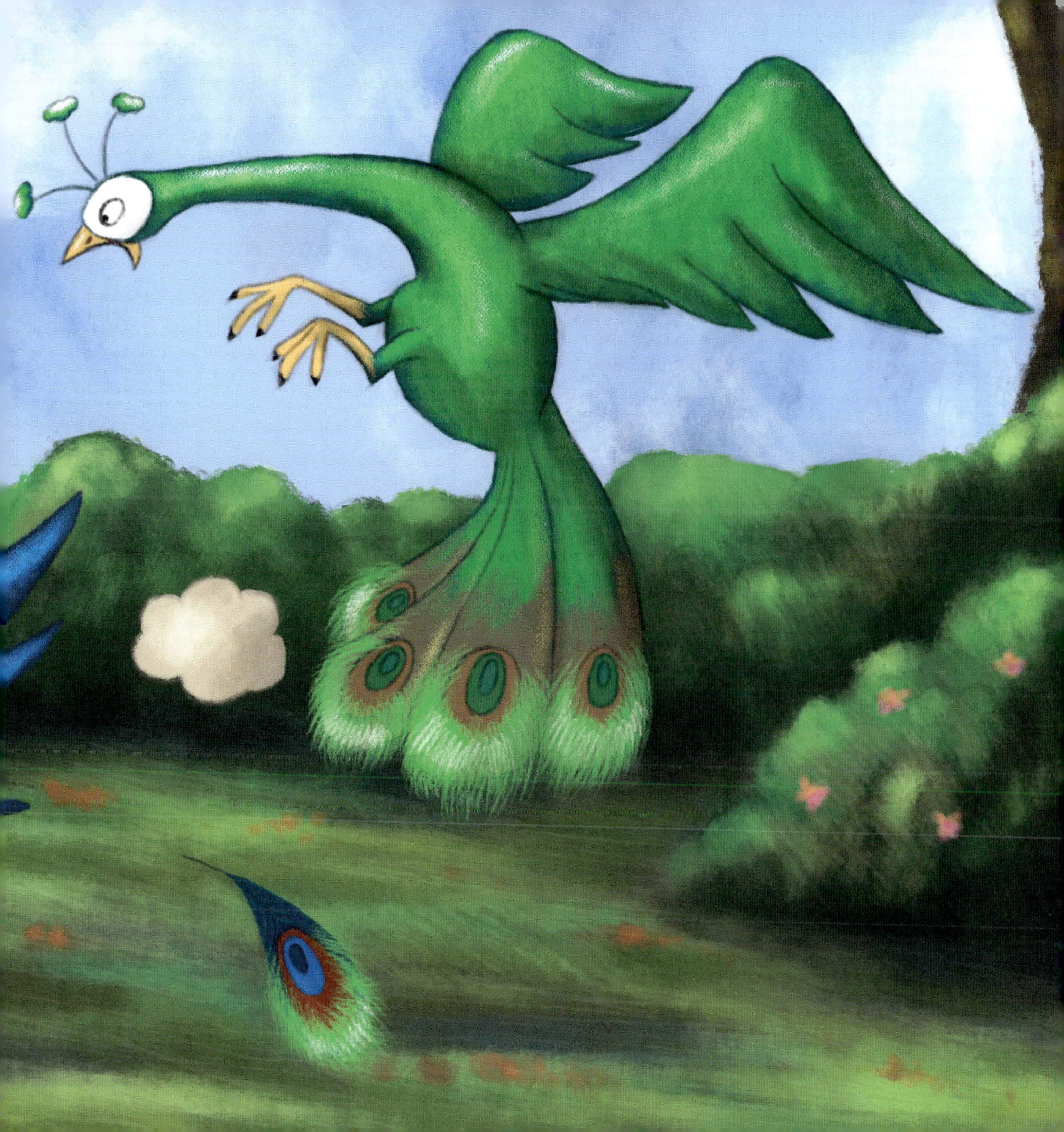

As they fought the fox together, some humans heard the commotion and came to their rescue. When the battle was over, the fox was gone but the older peacock was hurt. The humans took him away and the younger peacock didn't see him for days. When he saw him next, he had lost a lot of his feathers and they didn't look as beautiful as before.

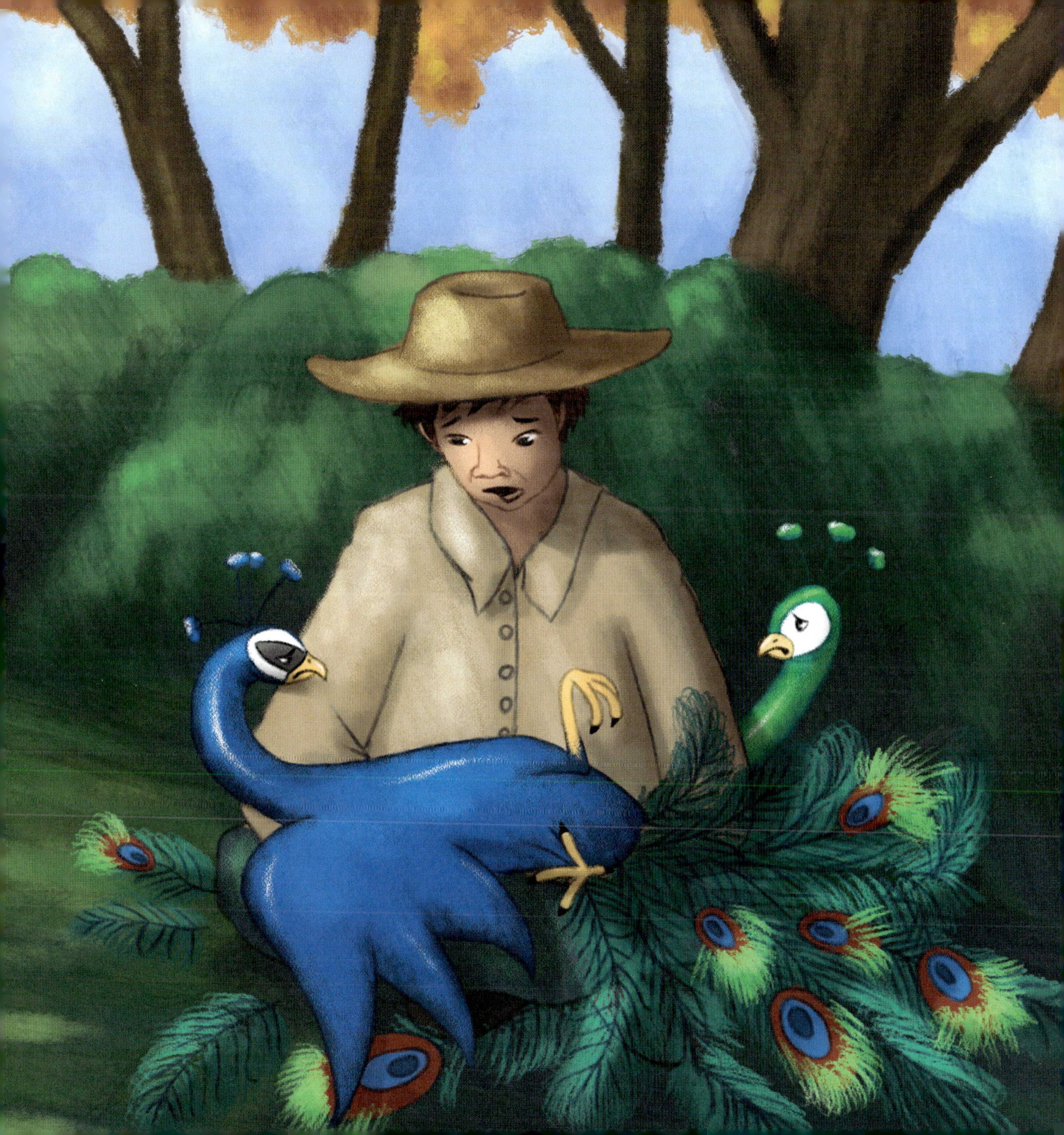

"What am I going to do now? Nobody will come to see me dance or even like me because I am so ugly.", cried the older peacock.

"I will like you no matter what." said the younger peacock. "I am your friend."

From that day on, the younger peacock and the older peacock were best friends. As time passed, the younger peacock grew up and he was very beautiful. Folks who had stopped coming to the garden started coming again to watch them both dance. But, none of that affected their friendship. They remained the best of friends and helped each other all their life.

Rohini Krishnapura

Rohini is the author of "Will you be my friend, peacock?" and "Mooli Stone Sambhar". She loves writing stories with an essence of India, where she was born. She's lived in the US for more than 20 years in various places including Nebraska, California, and now lives in Northern Virginia with her husband, two kids and their retriever. She founded boxinthemiddle LLC (https://boxinthemiddle.com) with a mission to nurture the love of learning and writing in children. In her day job, she uses her storytelling skills to help build better products by looking at data and creating a vision for the team.

Printed in Great Britain
by Amazon